S0-AGB-517

SPAIN

GROLIER
EDUCATIONAL

Published 1999 by Grolier Educational
Sherman Turnpike, Danbury, Connecticut.
Copyright © 1999 Times Editions Pte Ltd. Singapore.

Set ISBN: 0-7172-9324-6
Volume ISBN: 0-7172-9338-6

CIP information available from the Library of Congress or the publisher

Brown Partworks Ltd.

Series Editor: Tessa Paul
Series Designer: Joyce Mason
Crafts devised and created by Susan Moxley
Music arrangements by Harry Boteler
Photographs by Bruce Mackie
Production: Alex Mackenzie
Stylists: Joyce Mason and Tessa Paul

For this volume:
Writer: Irena Hoare
Consultant: Alejandro Vázquez, Instituto Cervantes, London.
Editorial Assistants: Hannah Beardon and Paul Thompson

Printed in Italy

Adult supervision advised for all crafts and recipes,
particularly those involving sharp instruments and heat.

CONTENTS

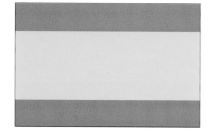

SPAIN:

Spain is situated in southwestern Europe and has coastlines on the Atlantic Ocean and the Mediterranean Sea.

▲ **La Sagrada Família,** or The Church of the Holy Family, is one of the most famous buildings in Spain. Designed by the architect Antoní Gaudí (1852–1926), its colorful, decorated spires tower over the city of Barcelona.

River Ebro

Spain

MADRID

River Tagus

Portugal

River Guadalquivir

Seville

El Rocio

Atlantic Ocean

Morocco

▶**The Spanish landscape** is renowned for its color and its rugged beauty. The hot sun on the Mediterranean coast enables grapes, olives, and almonds to be grown. Farmers on the windswept plains inland raise animals and grow grain.

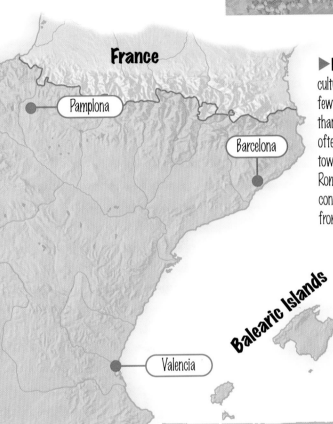

France

Pamplona

Barcelona

Balearic Islands

Valencia

Mt. Mulhacén

Mediterranean Sea

▶**Religion** is still a strong cultural force in Spain, although fewer people go to church now than in the past. Churches are often the finest buildings in towns and cities, and the Roman Catholic Church continues to receive money from the state.

First Impressions

- **Population** 39,417,220
- **Largest city** Madrid with a population of 2,909,792
- **Longest river** River Ebro
- **Highest mountain** Mt. Mulhacén (highest on mainland), at 11,475 ft.
- **Exports** Vehicles, fruit and vegetables, footwear, textiles, olive oil, and cork
- **Capital city** Madrid
- **Political status** Democratic monarchy
- **Climate** Varies from mild and wet in the north to hot and dry in the south
- **Art and culture** Three of the greatest painters in Western art were Spanish — Goya, Velázquez, and Picasso.

RELIGIONS

The Christian religion and the Roman Catholic Church are important in everyday Spanish life. The church is less powerful than it used to be, but Saints' days and the main events in the life of Jesus are celebrated in colorful festivals all over Spain.

CHRISTIANITY came to Spain at the time when the country was part of the Roman Empire. By the time the days of the empire were finally over, about 500 years after the death of Christ, Spain was rich in fine churches and cathedrals, all built for the glory of God. Some of these buildings can still be seen today.

Civil wars raged as the Roman Empire crumbled, and this allowed the Moors to invade Spain in A.D. 711. These Moors came from northern Africa and they were Muslims – followers of the religion of Islam.

Soon the Christian churches were mixed up with Arab mosques. These and other Moorish buildings can still be seen in many parts of Spain. Trade and culture flourished, and Christians were free to follow their own religion.

The Spanish Christians gradually started to reclaim their land. In 1492 the last Moors were chased from Spain. A royal family ruled the country, but they, and the people, were heavily controlled by the Roman Catholic Church. In the 1930s a fierce civil war raged through Spain. The old social system broke down. The royal family lost its position but the church retained its power for another 40 years. The Spanish people now live in a democracy with the monarch as head of state. There are over 60,000 churches in Spain, but Christianity is no longer taught in all the schools.

There is a small number of Spanish people who are Muslim or Jewish. Spain is a liberal country, and everyone is allowed to worship as they like.

GREETINGS FROM **SPAIN!**

Spain is the third largest country in Europe, with a population of over 39,000,000 people. The country has always been split into regions, each with its own capital city. It is like a collection of several small Spanish states. Each has its customs, and many speak their own dialects. The most common is Castilian, and this is what is usually called Spanish. Another language that is widely spoken is Catalan. Galego is spoken in the northwest. Euskera is used by the Basques in the north of the country. Spain once ruled over large areas of the Americas and parts of Africa. As a result, Spanish became the common language for numerous South American people. When these people broke away from Spanish rule, they kept Spanish as their official language.

How do you say...

Hello

¡Hola!

How are you?

¿Como estás?

My name is

Me llamo

Goodbye

Adios

Thank you

Gracias

Peace

La paz

7

SEMANA SANTA

Every year Christians all over the world remember the last week in the life of Jesus Christ. This is Easter week. In Spain it is called **Semana Santa,** *meaning "Holy Week."*

On the first day of Holy Week Jesus rode on a donkey into the city of Jerusalem. This city is now in modern Israel, but then it was part of the Roman Empire. The crowds cheered Jesus and waved palm leaves to greet Him as He passed by. The day is now remembered as Palm Sunday.

However, Jewish leaders mistrusted Jesus, and they asked the Roman authorities to arrest Him. The soldiers

Statues of Mary are draped in black lace during Holy Week. She is in mourning for her son Jesus. These statues may be surrounded by candles and carried through the streets at Easter.

In the Palm Sunday parades people carry palm leaves held by purple ribbons. Penitents may wear deep purple, and the churches drape purple over statues. It is the color of royalty and is used in churches on very holy days. Spring flowers are scattered over saints' statues.

mocked Jesus. They put a crown of thorns on His head, and beat Him. On the day that is now known as Good Friday soldiers forced Jesus to carry His cross to the hill where He was crucified.

It is a Christian belief that three days after the death of Jesus, He came back to life. This is called the Resurrection.

All these things are remembered during *Semana Santa* in Spain. People hang black cloths over balconies to show that they are

mourning the death of the Son of God, and there are many solemn processions with huge crowds taking part. Often the people in the crowds and in the parades dress up in clothes like those worn in the time of Jesus. Some also wear heavy, hooded robes.

Certain marchers come as "penitents," people who undertake a difficult task to show they are sorry for any bad acts. Penitents wear tall pointed hats and masks to cover their faces, and long robes. Some struggle under the

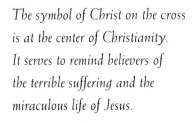

The symbol of Christ on the cross is at the center of Christianity. It serves to remind believers of the terrible suffering and the miraculous life of Jesus.

great burden of a heavy cross. They are experiencing Christ's suffering. Statues of Jesus and other holy figures are carried through villages and towns. The faithful kneel in the streets as these pass by.

As Good Friday approaches, Spanish men take part in an impressive ceremony called *Los Tamborados.* In solemn procession they beat drums for hours to demonstrate their mourning for Christ. Even when the drummers get tired, they do not stop the rhythmic drumming.

Good Friday is the day of Jesus Christ's crucifixion. No candles are lit in the church on Good Friday or Holy Saturday since these are the days when the faithful are mourning the death of Jesus.

RITUALS OF EASTER SUNDAY

Age-old rituals are part of the joy of Easter Sunday in Spain. Different regions have different ways of celebrating the festival. In some places festive bonfires are topped with a straw figure of Judas, the man who betrayed Jesus, and it goes up in flames as the fire blazes.

There is another ceremony, called the "descent of the angel," when a child dressed as an angel is carefully let down from a window on a rope, as if he or she is flying. The child, poised in the air, then lifts the black veil of mourning off the face of a statue of Mary.

SAETA

So - lo eres tu mi can - tar————

No pue - do can - tar ni quie - ro

a es - te Je - sus del man - de - ro Si - no á él

qu'an - du - vo en la mar.————

The "Saeta," based on a poem by Antonio Machado

I cannot sing, nor do I want to
To that Jesus on the cross
But rather to the One that walked on water.

On Easter Sunday a very special candle is lit in the churches. This is to symbolize Christ's victory over death. The sad time is over, and people gather together to enjoy a festive meal.

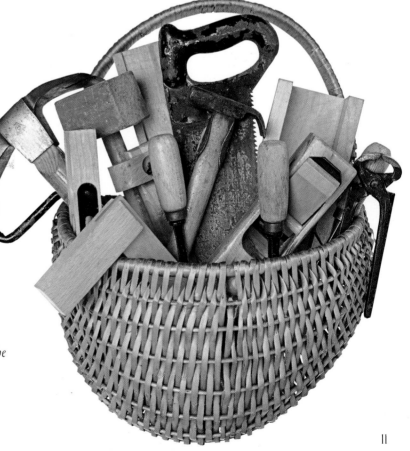

Boys carry carpenters' tools during the Holy Week parades in some towns. This is because such tools were used to make the cross of crucifixion, and also because Jesus was a carpenter by trade.

FERIA DEL ABRIL

The April Fair is often called the Horse Fair because it was once a market where people bought horses. These days the horses take part in colorful parades.

Seville is famous for its *Feria del Abril* – the "April Fair" – that lasts for six noisy, fun-filled days. It is held two weeks after Easter, at the start of the bullfighting season in Spain.

Although it was once a horse market, the fiesta has now become a wonderful excuse to have good meals and parties.

During the fair life in Seville moves to the fairground across the Guadalquivir River. Families and groups set up brightly colored tents called *caselas*, and people sit in them to eat, drink, make merry, and receive friends.

There is a special ceremony at the start of the April Fair when the whole fairground is lit up to signal the start of the festival. There is a party air, and everyone dances to the rhythm of the *flamenco*. This is the

Castanets are wooden clappers held in the hand. The clack of castanets and the hard tapping of feet create the rhythm of flamenco.

The Spanish are great horsemen, and the fair celebrates these noble beasts. The skill, speed, and beauty of the horse is on show. The riders also display their skills.

traditional dance of Spain and Seville.

In the mornings people stroll and admire the riders exercising their horses. In the afternoons the parades take over. The highlights are the elegant riders on horseback and the old carriages drawn by splendid horses.

Later still there is bullfighting, and the pace quickens. Night falls and the noise increases, while bright lanterns blaze against the dark sky.

MAKE A FAN

Fans were invented to keep people cool. However, they quickly became decorative and even fashionable. They were also used in ceremonies.

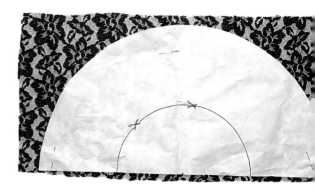

YOU WILL NEED
Large sheet of cardboard
Sheet of tracing paper
⅓ yard of black lace
Black embroidery thread
Pencil, compass, and scissors
Craft glue
Paint

1 Draw a semicircle of 10" radius onto cardboard with compass. Using same center, draw a semicircle of 5" radius. Copy the semicircles onto tracing paper. Pin tracing paper onto lace. Cut around outer and inner radius to make a curved strip of lace.

2 Cut 9 cardboard strips, each 10½" x ½". Pierce a hole in each strip 1" from one end. Paint strips. For tassel, wind embroidery thread around 2" wide cardboard. Slip off cardboard. Tie threads close to one end, then snip through loop at other end. Tie another thread around the tassel and thread it through holes in strips. Make a knot.

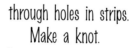

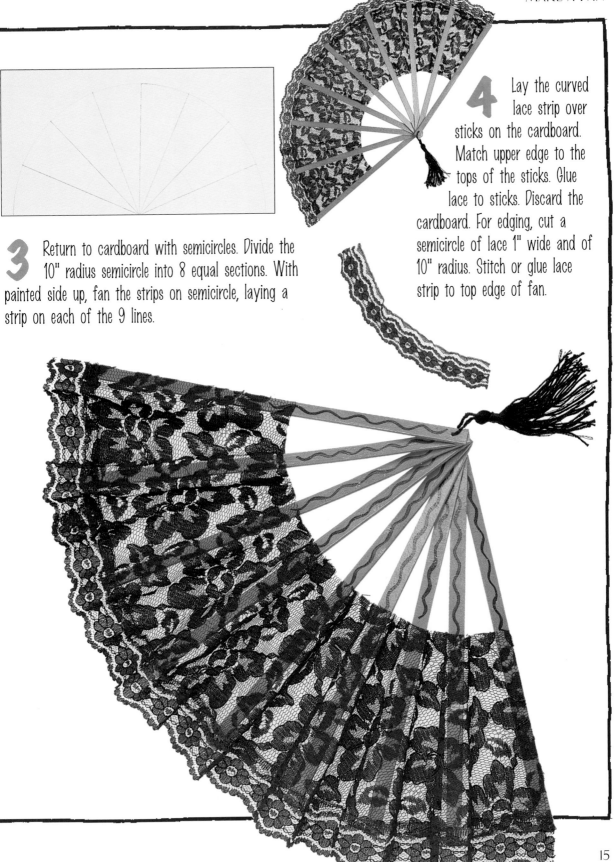

4 Lay the curved lace strip over sticks on the cardboard. Match upper edge to the tops of the sticks. Glue lace to sticks. Discard the cardboard. For edging, cut a semicircle of lace 1" wide and of 10" radius. Stitch or glue lace strip to top edge of fan.

3 Return to cardboard with semicircles. Divide the 10" radius semicircle into 8 equal sections. With painted side up, fan the strips on semicircle, laying a strip on each of the 9 lines.

LAS FALLAS

*In the Spanish city of Valencia the start of spring is marked by the Festival of the Great Fire. In Spain this festival is called **Las Fallas de San José**.*

The joyous Festival of the Great Fire lasts for a week between March 13 and 19 in Valencia.

The first Fallas fires were lit in medieval times. They signaled the end of winter and celebrated San José's – Saint Joseph's – Day on March 19. The fires were lit on top of tall wooden masts, so people were able to see them from far off. The boys of Valencia began to make models of the townspeople they did not like and then burned the models at Las Fallas. The people of Valencia continue

Saint Joseph, or San José, the earthly parent to Jesus, is the patron saint of carpenters. Carpenters used to celebrate his day, March 19, by burning their workroom rubbish on the Fallas fires. Now offerings of flowers are laid around statues of Joseph.

this tradition and build models of those they want to tease. The models are called *ninots*, and there is fierce competition to make the grandest ninot. The best one each year is stored in a museum, but all the rest are burned.

Each afternoon there is a fireworks display in the Plaza del Ayuntamiento. This is a signal for the start of street processions, many led by the Fallas Queen. People in masks or folk costumes dance in the streets.

The last night of the festival is the "night of fire." The ninots are made into one huge monument, the *falla*. At midnight this is set alight, causing a huge bonfire. Fireworks are let off to light up the night sky.

The Fallas Queen wears gorgeous golden combs in her hair and covers her shoulders with fine embroidered and fringed shawls.

GAZPACHO

SERVES SIX
1 cucumber, peeled, seeded, and diced
3 lbs. tomatoes, peeled and cut in half crosswise
½ red onion, finely chopped
½ red pepper, diced
8 oz. V8 juice
¼ cup finely chopped parsley
1 t. salt
½ t. pepper
2 T. fresh lime juice
1 t. sugar
1 cup garlic croutons

To deseed the tomatoes, place a large sieve over a bowl, then squeeze out the seeds over the sieve. Save the juice but discard seeds. Purée half the tomatoes in a food processor. Chop the other half. Put all the ingredients, including the reserved tomato juice, in a large bowl and stir well. Cover and refrigerate for one hour. Serve garnished with croutons.

SAINT JOSEPH

Saint Joseph, the earthly father of Jesus, was visited in his dreams by angels who were sent from God. They helped Joseph to keep Jesus safe from harm.

ONCE THERE WAS a carpenter called Joseph who was able to make all sorts of things out of wood. He lived in the town of Nazareth in Judea, and he was engaged to a girl called Mary.

One day Joseph was tired so he lay down to rest in a field. While he slept, he dreamed that a bright angel came to him. The angel told him that Mary was going to have a baby. He told Joseph that the baby must be called Jesus and that this baby was the Son of God. It was Joseph's mission to protect the boy.

Joseph and Mary were pleased a baby was to be born to them and made happy plans for Him.

Some time later the king, whose name was Herod, gave an order. Everyone had to go to the town where they had been born and report to the authorities. Herod wanted to count all his subjects. Now, Joseph came from Bethlehem so he had to go there with his wife, Mary.

They made the long journey with Mary riding on a donkey. At last they reached the town of Bethlehem. All the inns were full of people. "No room at the inn" was all they heard. A kind innkeeper let them rest in his stable where his farm animals were housed. Jesus was born with the gentle animals watching over Him.

Wise men and shepherds visited

the baby. They called Him the Son of God and the King of Kings. This was told to King Herod and it made him very angry. He ordered soldiers to kill all the boy babies in Bethlehem and in the whole country. Even as Herod issued this dreadful order, Joseph dreamed of an angel.

The angel told him his family was in danger. Joseph woke up, gathered the Child in his arms, and fled with Mary to Egypt.

They felt safe in this foreign land, but they were very pleased when the angel came to Joseph once more. He told Joseph that Herod was dead and that it was safe to return to Judea. So Joseph took Mary and Jesus on the long road back to Nazareth.

Joseph taught Jesus the trade of the carpenter. All through Jesus's childhood Joseph was a loyal guardian to the Son of God.

19

ROMERIA DE ROCIO

Romeria de Rocio *means the "pilgrimage to El Rocio." It occurs at Whitsun, when Christians celebrate the appearance of the Holy Spirit on Earth. This festival also honors the Virgin Mary.*

Every year at this time pilgrims pour into the tiny town of El Rocio in Andalusia in northern Spain. Pilgrims are those who visit holy places. They go to El Rocio to worship at the Church of Nuestra Senora del Rocio where there is a famous statue of Mary, the mother of Jesus Christ.

The statue is centuries old, and people believe it can perform miracles. A miracle is an event that goes against the laws of nature. It is said that this Virgin heals illness.

Although Christ died on the cross, Christians believe He came back to life. They also believe the Holy Spirit came down to Earth. Carts are decorated to honor the Virgin and the Holy Spirit.

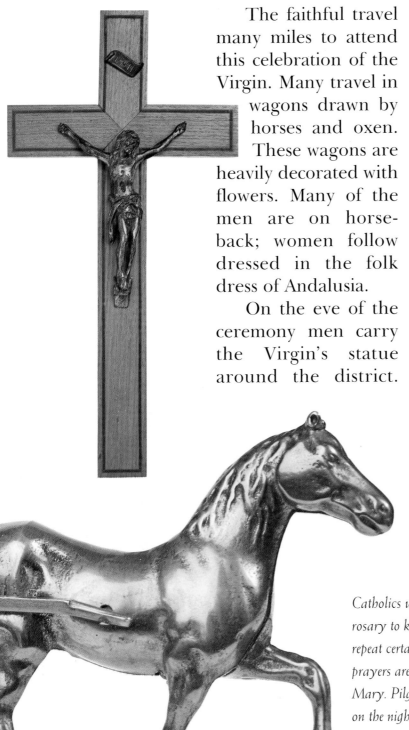

The faithful travel many miles to attend this celebration of the Virgin. Many travel in wagons drawn by horses and oxen.

These wagons are heavily decorated with flowers. Many of the men are on horseback; women follow dressed in the folk dress of Andalusia.

On the eve of the ceremony men carry the Virgin's statue around the district.

Pilgrims follow carrying candles. As the crowd moves solemnly through the night, it is accompanied by the constant sound of singing, flutes, and tambourines.

The archbishop of Seville, a very senior priest, blesses the Virgin. Many pilgrims struggle to touch this image of the Virgin as it is carried about. Catholics believe the Virgin Mary takes their prayers and wishes to God. They ask her for favors. Dances and parties are held after church.

Catholics use the beads of the rosary to keep count as they repeat certain prayers. The prayers are to Jesus or the Virgin Mary. Pilgrims carry a rosary on the night march in El Rocio.

MAKE A STRAW DONKEY

The first toys were probably made of straw, and then of clay. This donkey is constructed from wire and straw, and carries some clay water jugs. He also wears a fabric saddle and wool harness. The straw donkey looks charming on a kitchen or bedroom shelf.

Donkeys have played a role in human life for centuries. They are small, and they do not eat huge amounts of food, so they are cheap to keep. They are, however, strong enough to carry burdens and people. Donkeys are also patient beasts. They are rarely aggressive and are safe for children to handle.

In Mediterranean countries, such as Spain, the donkey is slowly being replaced by motorcycles or little three-wheeled motor vehicles. However, in mountainous villages or over rough country where roads are not made for cars the donkey is still very useful. They are often loaded with pottery jugs that keep wine and water cool in the hot Spanish sun.

YOU WILL NEED

1 yard thin wire
Bag of soft straw
Ball of raffia
Scrap of felt
Short length of wool
Modeling clay
Bundle of twigs

1 Twist a wire frame for the donkey by making a cylinder, curved into a neck/head shape at one end, with four stems for legs. Pull a handful of straw into a sausage shape. Starting at one leg, twist and shape straw over entire frame. Bind the straw into place with raffia.

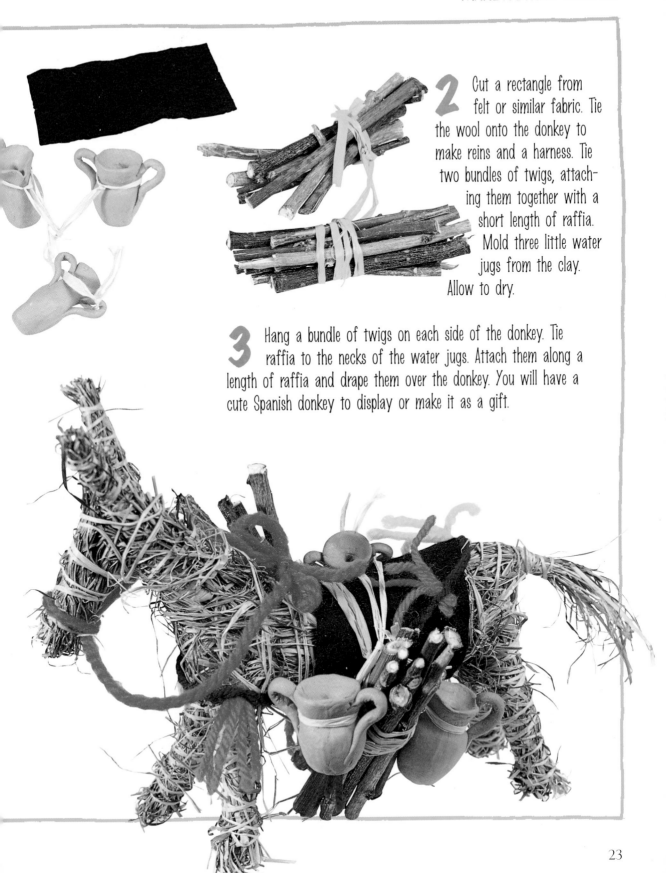

2 Cut a rectangle from felt or similar fabric. Tie the wool onto the donkey to make reins and a harness. Tie two bundles of twigs, attaching them together with a short length of raffia. Mold three little water jugs from the clay. Allow to dry.

3 Hang a bundle of twigs on each side of the donkey. Tie raffia to the necks of the water jugs. Attach them along a length of raffia and drape them over the donkey. You will have a cute Spanish donkey to display or make it as a gift.

23

SAN FERMÍN

The festival of San Fermín, named after the patron saint of bullfighters, is a celebration of their sport. These festivals happen all over Spain, but the fiesta in Pamplona is the most famous one.

People are out on the streets at all hours during the noisy festival of San Fermín in Pamplona. The fiesta goes on for eight hectic days from July 6.

Each day is begun by musicians with pipes and drums, who set off from the City Hall to wind through the city streets.

In one parade a great silver statue of San Fermín is taken through the streets. It is followed by people in huge plaster heads.

Another parade demonstrates the great importance of the old sport of bullfighting. Riders who help in the bullrings gallop out dressed in black capes and hats adorned with white plumes. They are followed by their

A matador has two capes. One is for wearing, and the other — a smaller, red one — is used to attract the bull. The matador's sequin-covered suit is called the trajedo di luca, which means the "suit of lights."

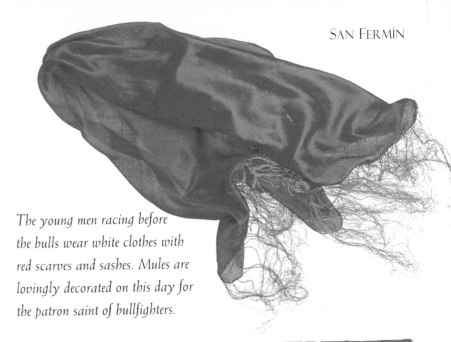

The young men racing before the bulls wear white clothes with red scarves and sashes. Mules are lovingly decorated on this day for the patron saint of bullfighters.

mules, which are also honored for their role in the bullfight.

A rocket is fired to signal that the bulls are to be let out of their pens. The bulls charge down narrow streets to the bullring. Daring young men race ahead of them. This bull-running is called the *encierro*.

The evenings are for bullfights. The matadors are greeted by crowds who throw flowers into the arena or wave handkerchiefs to show approval for the matadors' skill.

POTATO FRITTATA

SERVES SIX
4 large potatoes
2 fl. oz. olive oil
4 eggs
4 fl. oz. water
Salt and pepper

Slice the potato very thinly with a sharp knife, on the wide blade of a grater, or in a good food processor. Ask an adult to help you. Heat the oil in a large frying pan. Add the potatoes to the pan, being careful not to splash yourself with hot oil. Cook, turning occasionally for 10 to 15 minutes until soft. Whisk the eggs, water, salt, and pepper together. Add to the potatoes and cook until the bottom is set. To cook the top, place under a pre-heated grill for 3 to 5 minutes. Cut into six slices and serve.

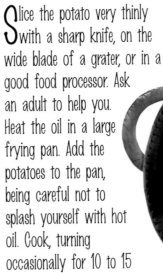

25

SAINT FIRMINUS, AN EARLY MARTYR

Saint Firminus is the English name for San Fermín. He is thought to protect bullfighters, and he is also the guardian of Pamplona.

THERE WAS ONCE a rich and important senator in the Spanish town of Pamplona. At that time the Romans ruled Spain, and all the people worshipped Roman gods.

One day the senator and his wife, Eugenia, were on their way to worship at the temple of Jupiter, the Roman god. When they reached the temple, they were surprised by the sound of a loud voice and the sight of a small crowd.

The senator asked someone to explain what was going on. They were told it was the voice of Honestus and that he was talking about his god, Jesus Christ.

The senator and Eugenia stopped to listen to the preacher, and they argued with him in favor of their old gods. Honestus told his new friends to come and meet his master, Saturnius. He was a very clever teacher who would teach them the truth of Christianity. Sure enough, the couple went to meet Saturnius, and he turned them from the old Roman gods. They became followers of Jesus Christ.

Now the senator and Eugenia wanted their son, Firminus, to be taught by Honestus. Firminus went to live with Honestus. Together they walked through Spain and also France.

Everywhere on their long journey, they talked about Jesus. Often, while traveling on short treks between villages, they were joined by many people who wanted to learn about Jesus.

Firminus was so quick to learn that before long he was a preacher too. He became the first bishop of Amiens, in France. A bishop is a very important priest. However, his life was not easy. There were many who were angered by Firminus's beliefs and they thought the religion of the people should be the same as the religion of the Romans. Because of this they plotted to kill Firminus. They trapped him and cut off his head.

They killed him because he did not believe in their gods. This made Firminus one of the first Christian martyrs. A martyr is a person who dies for his or her faith.

CHRISTMAS

Christmas is a Christian holiday that celebrates the birth of Jesus. In Spain the festivities end with Epiphany 12 days after Christmas.

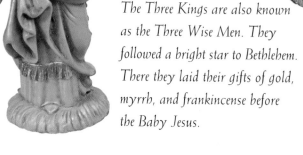

Spanish families get together for the birth of Jesus on Christmas Eve, or *Nochebueno*. Friends and families meet for an evening meal, then they all go to church for Midnight Mass. In Spanish this Mass is called the *Misa del Gallo*, meaning the "Mass of the Rooster." According to an old folk tale, this bird was the first living creature to announce the birth of Jesus Christ.

Afterward people spill out of their churches. They are in a party mood and set off fireworks.

Spanish churches are specially decorated

The Three Kings are also known as the Three Wise Men. They followed a bright star to Bethlehem. There they laid their gifts of gold, myrrh, and frankincense before the Baby Jesus.

for Christmas, as are churches everywhere. Flickering candles and colored lights glow. There is always a nativity scene, called a *nacimiento*, on display. This is a model of

Baby Jesus in His crib, with Joseph and Mary, and the animals that were in the stable where He was born.

Some churches may have a nativity scene with real people in it

SWEET FEAST

Christmas is celebrated with festive food. The Spanish feast on special breads, cakes, and nougat called *turron.*. These might contain aniseed, cinnamon, sesame, almonds, or sweet wine. They have a spicy, oriental flavor, showing the tastes the Moors brought to Spanish food. It is thought, however, that eating sweet food at this time is a pre-Christian custom. In Roman times, before the birth of Christ, such foods were meant to promise a sweet and happy new year. Dried fruits are piled in serving bowls to be offered to guests who visit over the holiday period. The turron are served with coffee and liqueurs after a meal or with the sparkling Spanish wine called Cava. The children have fruit juices.

dressed up as Mary and Joseph, and as angels, kings, and shepherds. In other places local people act out the nativity story in their church.

It is very common for families in Spain to have model nativity scenes in their homes. Many families inherit antique scenes of great beauty, and these are brought out each year. During the festivities children dance around the nacimiento and adults play the guitar or tambourine.

Children in Spain receive presents on the day when it is said that the Three Kings brought their gifts to Jesus. This day is called Epiphany, and it happens on the twelfth day after Christmas.

The children put their shoes out on a balcony, or a window ledge, on the night before Epiphany. They also leave food for the camels that the Three Kings traveled upon to visit Baby Jesus. The children hope to find presents in their shoes.

In many towns people dress up as the Three Kings and parade the streets on horseback. They throw candy to the children.

On the eve of Epiphany rows of small shoes can be seen on windowsills. The Three Wise Men tuck presents into the footwear!

29

RECONQUISTAS

Starting from about A.D. 700 Moors from Africa conquered most of Spain. They had control for nearly 500 years. They came across the Mediterranean Sea and tried to invade many ports and islands of the European coast. The battles against the Moors are remembered in festivals all over Spain.

The long fight to free Spain from the control of the Moors is called the *Reconquistas*. This struggle against the conqueror lasted hundreds of years and the many battles are still remembered. They are re-enacted in over 150 festivals across the country.

Local people dress in costumes as Moorish warriors. Others dress as Christian soldiers. They parade before a mock fortress or before old Moorish buildings. Captains tell each side to stop bad feelings between them. The crowd shouts, "No!" A mock battle takes place. Drums roll, bells ring, and muskets fire their blank shot. Fireworks add to the atmosphere of a medieval battle. Often there are fairs at the battleground. Farm produce and crafts are sold at stalls. The crowds dance to band music.

WORDS TO KNOW

Civil war: A war between citizens of the same country.

Dialect: A regional variety of a language.

Martyr: A person who is put to death for refusing to give up his or her faith.

Mass: A Christian ritual in which bread and wine are used to commemorate the Last Supper of Jesus Christ.

Medieval: To do with the Middle Ages.

Middle Ages: The period between the fifth and the fifteenth centuries.

Miracle: An event that goes against the laws of nature.

Moors: A Muslim people from northwest Africa who conquered Spain in the eighth century.

Mosque: A Muslim place of worship.

Muslim: A follower of the religion of Islam.

Patron saint: A saint who is special to a particular group. Nations, towns, and professions have patron saints.

Penitent: A person who performs difficult or painful tasks to make up for bad things that he or she has done.

Pilgrim: A person who makes a religious journey, or pilgrimage, to a holy place.

Resurrection: The rising of Christ from the dead on Easter Sunday.

Roman Catholic: A member of the Roman Catholic Church, the largest branch of Christianity. The head of this church is the pope.

Roman Empire: An empire stretches over a large area or many countries. It is ruled by one authority. At its height in the second century the Roman Empire covered much of Europe and North Africa, and a part of Asia.

Saint: A title given to very holy people by some Christian churches. Saints are important in the Roman Catholic Church.

ACKNOWLEDGMENTS

WITH THANKS TO:
Vale Antiques, London.
Catholic Truth Society Bookshop,
London. Pollock's Toy Museum,
London. Hourican's Public House,
London.

PHOTOGRAPHY:
All photographs by Bruce Mackie
except: John Elliott pp. 17, 25.
Marshall Cavendish p. 17
Cover photograph by Corbis/Paul
Thompson.

ILLUSTRATIONS BY:
Fiona Saunders pp. 4 – 5. Tracy Rich
p. 7. Alison Fleming p. 19. Maps by
John Woolford.

Recipes: Ellen Dupont.

Set Contents